GW01191002

04506029

AMAZING
Waterfalls
AROUND
THE WORLD

by Roxanne Troup

raintree

a Capstone company — publishers for children

Raintree is an imprint of Capstone Global Library Limited, a company incorporated in England and Wales having its registered office at 264 Banbury Road, Oxford, OX2 7DY – Registered company number: 6695582

www.raintree.co.uk
myorders@raintree.co.uk

Edited by Claire Vanden Branden
Designed by Becky Daum
Original illustrations © Capstone Global Library Limited 2020
Production by Dan Peluso
Originated by Capstone Global Library Ltd
Printed and bound in India

ISBN 978 1 4747 7470 3 (hardback)
ISBN 978 1 4747 8123 7 (paperback)

British Library Cataloguing in Publication Data
A full catalogue record for this book is available from the British Library.

Acknowledgements
We would like to thank the following for permission to reproduce photographs: iStockphoto: best-photo, 11, GoodOlga, 26–27, Indigoai, 7, Kamadie, 19, Serjio74, 8–9, vau902, 12–13; Shutterstock Images: Douglas Olivares, 16–17, Janelle Lugge, 25, Maridav, 5, 28, Michael Ransburg, 23, StanislavBeloglazov, 20–21, TRphotos, cover, Vadim Petrakov, 15, 31.

CONTENTS

CHAPTER 1

AMAZING Waterfalls

Water flows from high points to low points on Earth. It wears away soft rock and soil as it flows. Hard rock is left behind. This rock forms a sharp edge. Then water flows over the edge. This makes a waterfall. The water drops into a pool below.

Waterfalls can sound like a loud roar. Some can be seen from many kilometres away. Waterfalls can have some amazing features. Their mist can make rainforests. Discover some of the world's most amazing waterfalls.

Waterfalls can be found all over the world.

CHAPTER 2

NIAGARA Falls

Niagara Falls is the largest waterfall in North America. It has three different waterfalls. Its water comes from the Great Lakes. More than 159 million litres (45 million gallons) of water flow over the falls every minute.

Millions of people visit Niagara Falls every year.

8

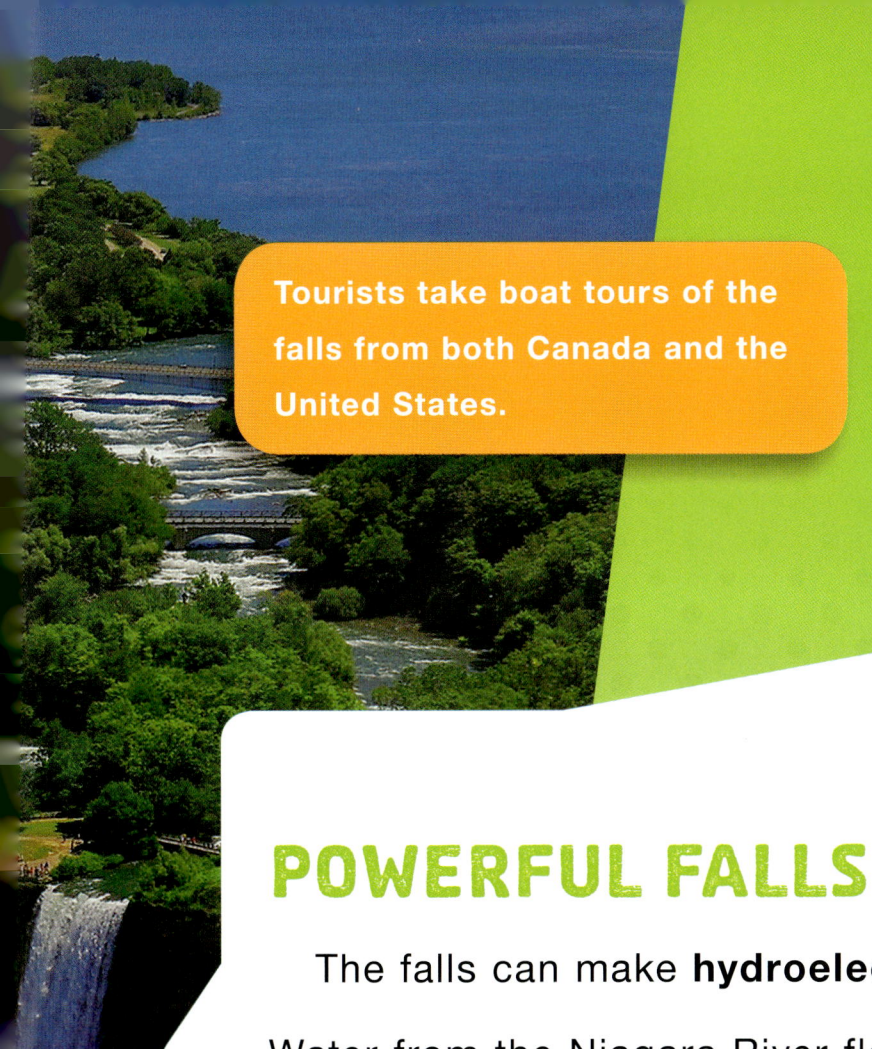

Tourists take boat tours of the falls from both Canada and the United States.

POWERFUL FALLS

The falls can make **hydroelectricity**. Water from the Niagara River flows into a dam. The water turns a **turbine** in a **generator**. The energy from the flowing water is changed into electricity.

CHAPTER 3

IGUAZÚ Falls

Iguazú Falls is in South America. The Iguazú River drops into a **canyon** called the Devil's Throat. It is shaped like a horseshoe. Water falls over its sides and forms 275 different waterfalls.

Iguazú means "big water" in the language of the local area.

The mist from the falls turned the area into a rainforest. Many different plants grow there. There are hundreds of different birds. Visitors might even see jaguars.

Iguazú Falls is on the border of Argentina and Brazil.

CHAPTER 4

ANGEL
Falls

Angel Falls in Venezuela is the tallest waterfall in the world. It is 979 metres (3,212 feet) high. During the **dry season**, not much water flows over the falls. It **evaporates** and seems to disappear in mid-air!

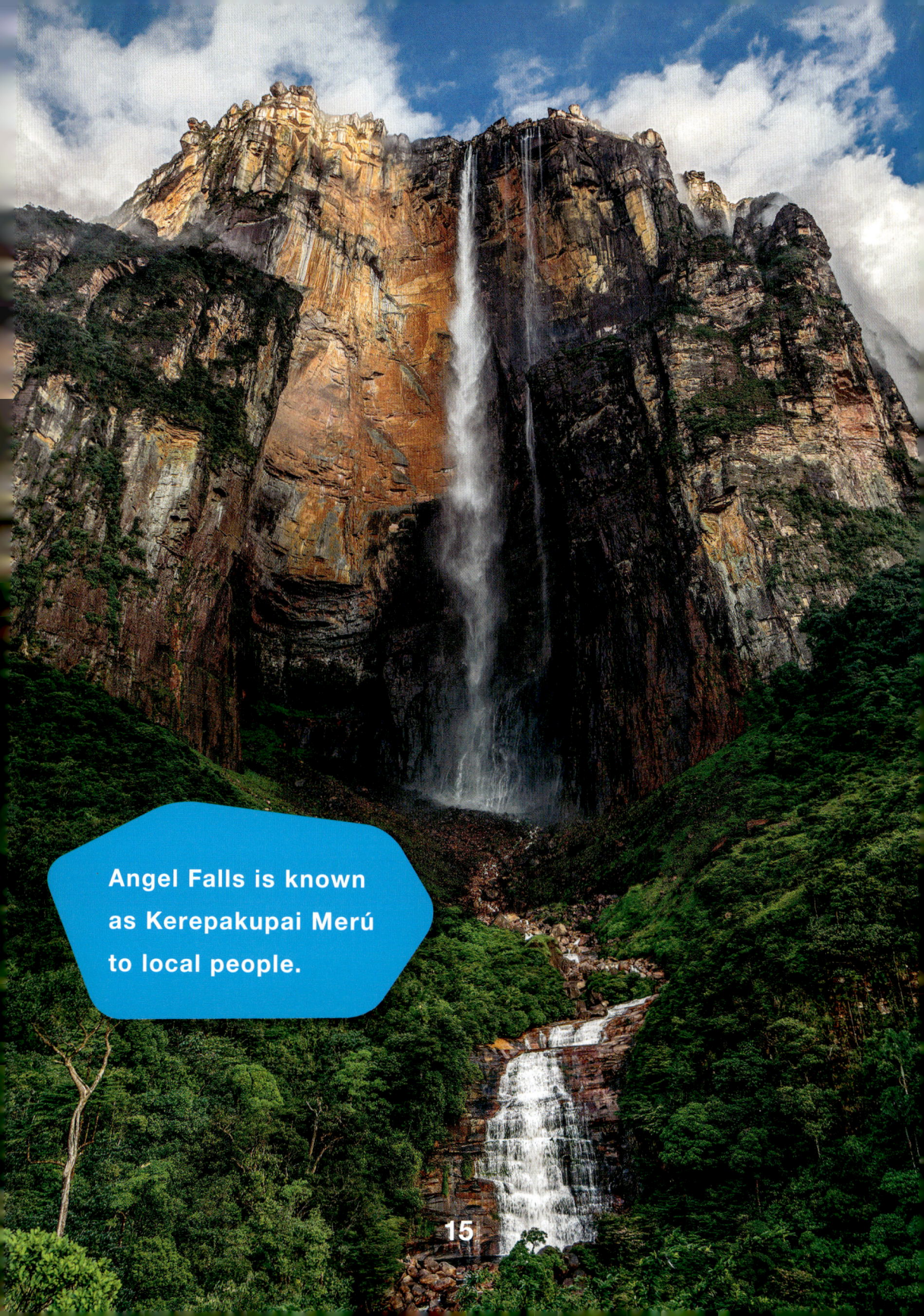

Angel Falls is known as Kerepakupai Merú to local people.

Angel Falls is hard to visit because it is in a jungle. There are no roads, so visitors see the falls by air or boat. Some people travel on foot to get a closer look.

DISCOVERED BY CHANCE

Angel Falls was found by accident. James Angel saw the falls from his plane in 1933. The falls were named after him. Only people local to the area knew about the falls before then.

Angel Falls is in Canaima National Park. Many visitors take canoes through the park to see the falls.

CHAPTER 5

VICTORIA
Falls

Victoria Falls is in Africa. It is twice as big as Niagara Falls. Visitors can see its spray from a few kilometres away. The spray looks like smoke.

Victoria Falls's local name is Mosi-oa-Tunya. It means "the smoke that thunders".

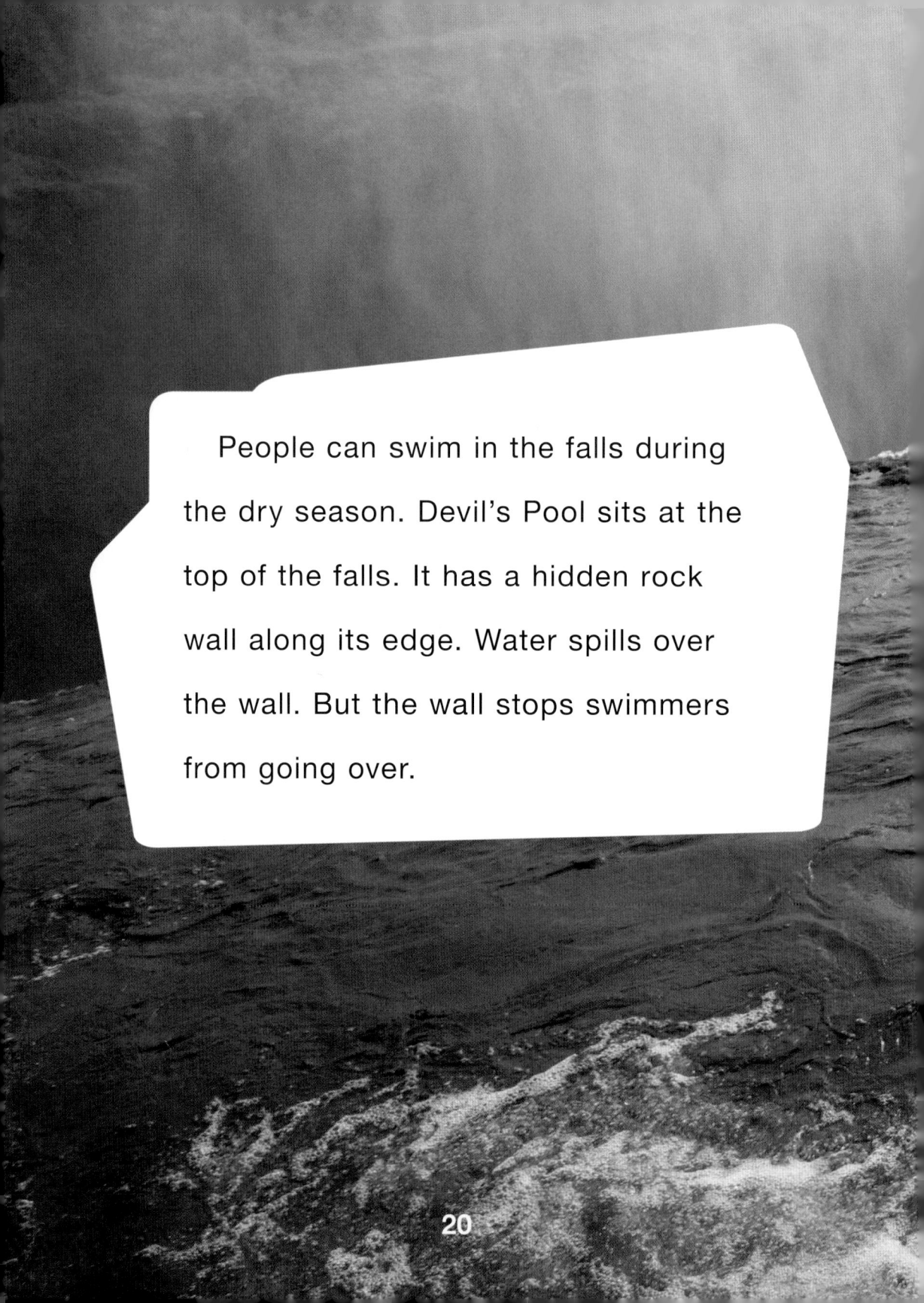

People can swim in the falls during the dry season. Devil's Pool sits at the top of the falls. It has a hidden rock wall along its edge. Water spills over the wall. But the wall stops swimmers from going over.

Visitors to Devil's Pool enjoy the view when they play in the water.

CHAPTER 6

GULLFOSS

Gullfoss is in Iceland. The water from this fall flows into a canyon. It drops between two **tectonic plates**. It looks as though it disappears into the earth.

GOLDEN FALLS

Gullfoss's name means "golden falls". The falls look gold in the sunshine.

Gullfoss has two separate waterfalls.

23

CHAPTER 7

UNUSUAL
Waterfalls

Horizontal Falls is in Talbot Bay, Australia. The falls are caused by ocean **tides**. Tides push water in and out of the bay. The water flows through a small opening and looks like a sideways waterfall.

UPSIDE-DOWN WATERFALL

Waipuhia Falls is in Hawaii, USA. It is an upside-down waterfall. The water doesn't really flow up. It just looks as though it does. Strong winds blow water up the mountain.

Horizontal Falls is nicknamed "the Horries".

UNDERWATER FALLS

Mauritius is off the coast of Africa.

It has a waterfall unlike any other.

But you can't visit it. It's underwater!

Mauritius and its underwater waterfall are in the Indian Ocean.

DENMARK STRAIT

The Denmark Strait has an actual underwater waterfall. It is more than 3 kilometes (2 miles) high. Nearly four billion litres (one billion gallons) of water flow over it per second.

It's not really a waterfall. It just looks like one from above. The sand movement under the ocean makes it look like water is falling.

GLOSSARY

canyon
deep valley with steep sides made when a river cuts through rock

dry season
time of year when there is no rain

evaporate
change from a liquid into steam or vapour

generator
machine that converts one form of energy into another

hydroelectricity
electricity made from running water

tectonic plate
large, slow-moving section of Earth's crust

tide
changing sea levels caused by the pull of the Moon

turbine
engine that is powered by water that passes through the blades of a wheel and makes it revolve

TOP WATERFALLS TO VISIT

ANGEL FALLS, VENEZUELA
Visit the highest waterfall in the world.

GULLFOSS, ICELAND
Travel to this golden waterfall.

HORIZONTAL FALLS, AUSTRALIA
Experience these sideways rapids.

IGUAZÚ FALLS, SOUTH AMERICA
Stop and see 275 waterfalls at once.

NIAGARA FALLS, NORTH AMERICA
See millions of gallons of water flow every minute.

UNDERWATER WATERFALL, MAURITIUS
See this underwater waterfall from the sky.

VICTORIA FALLS, AFRICA
See the biggest waterfall in the world.

WAIPUHIA FALLS, HAWAII, USA
Watch this waterfall appear to flow upwards.

ACTIVITY

MAKE YOUR OWN INDOOR WATERFALL!

Use water, vegetable oil and food colouring to make your own indoor waterfall.

WHAT YOU'LL NEED:

- tall drinking glass
- water
- bowl
- 1 tablespoon vegetable oil
- liquid food colouring
- fork

INSTRUCTIONS:

1. Fill your glass with water. It should be about three-quarters full.

2. Put 1 tablespoon of oil in your bowl.

3. Add several drops of food colouring to the bowl. Use as many colours as you like!

4. Use the fork to mix the food colouring in the bowl.

5. Pour the mixture from the bowl into the glass. Sit back and watch! The food colouring will make waterfalls inside the glass.

FIND OUT MORE

Books

Earth's Landforms (Earth By Numbers), Nancy Dickmann (Raintree, 2018)

Exploring Rivers: A Benjamin Blog and His Inquisitive Dog Investigation (Exploring Habitats with Benjamin Blog and His Inquisitive Dog), Anita Ganeri (Raintree, 2015)

Waterfall Watchers (Landform Adventurers), Pam Rosenberg (Raintree, 2011)

Websites

www.bbc.com/bitesize/articles/z7w8pg8
Learn more about rivers.

www.dkfindout.com/uk/earth/rivers/waterfalls-and-rapids
Find out more about waterfalls and rapids.

INDEX